The Risen Savior

LIVING IN THE POWER OF CHRIST'S RESURRECTION

DR. JOHN ANIEMEKE
DR. CHIDINMA ANIEMEKE

THE RISEN SAVIOR
Living in the Power of Christ's Resurrection

Copyright ©2025 by Dr. John Aniemeke & Dr. Chidinma Aniemeke

Paperback ISBN: 978-1-965593-38-7

All rights reserved. No part of this publication may be reproduced, distributed, or transmitted in any form or by any means, including photocopying, recording, or other electronic or mechanical methods without the prior written permission of the authors except in the case of brief quotations embodied in reviews and certain other non-commercial uses permitted by copyright law.

Published by Cornerstone Publishing

A Division of Cornerstone Creativity Group LLC
Info@thecornerstonepublishers.com
www.thecornerstonepublishers.com

Author's Contact

To book the authors to speak at your next event or to order bulk copies of this book, please, use the information below:

janiemeke@yahoo.com

Printed in the United States of America.

FOREWORD

I have had the privilege of reviewing the contents of this book, The Risen Savior. Ever since, I have continually prayed that it serves as a conduit for the fulfillment of God's redemptive provisions in people's lives. This book speaks to the reality of restoration—whether it be the triumph of a believer after many trials, the comeback of a sportsman in the final moments, the revival of hope for a politician, or the miraculous resurrection of what seemed lost, much like the dry bones in Ezekiel's vision.

The Risen Savior is a profound exposition of God's redemptive plan—a divine blueprint set in motion from the very fall of man in the Garden of Eden. In the grand narrative of restoration, Jesus Christ, the Savior, stands as the central figure. As man's substitute, He took on the mission of redemption, living a sinless life in defiance of the enemy, surrendering His body and blood on the Cross to atone for humanity's sins, and ultimately embracing burial. Yet, in divine recompense, He triumphed through the Resurrection, securing eternal righteousness and victory for all who believe. This book is a celebration of that victory—a testament to the life of dominion found in Christ.

The message of The Risen Savior highlights the Resurrection of Jesus as the cornerstone of our faith. Through unwavering faith in Him, believers partake in His victory and dominion, empowered by the Holy Spirit to live in the fullness of divine life. The atonement at Calvary and the Resurrection are the twin pillars upon which the Christian faith stands, and this book masterfully underscores their significance. I wholeheartedly recommend The Risen Savior to all who seek a deeper revelation of Christ's victory.

I am also deeply honored to be affiliated with the co-authors of this book—true vessels of God's Kingdom. Their unwavering dedication to Christ and their commitment to spreading the message of His Resurrection set them apart as torchbearers of this generation. The words within these pages, born from their hearts and divine inspiration, will impart grace, favor, and anointing to you as you embrace the power of the Resurrection Life—one filled with breakthroughs, wonders, and the manifest glory of God.

Apostle Emmanuel E. Nwogu

The Apostolic Church, Brooklyn, NY

DEDICATION

This book is dedicated to the Glory of God and to all believers in Christ who long for His return. Maranatha!

CONTENTS

INTRODUCTION vii

1. The Great Proclamation: He Is Risen! 1

2. Proofs Of The Resurrection 11

3. Crucifixion: The Beginning Of Resurrection Blessings 31

4. The Wonders Of Christ's Death 39

5. The Resurrection As The Cornerstone Of Our Faith .. 51

6. The Resurrection And Your Dominion 67

7. The Resurrection And Our Eternal Glory 83

CONCLUSION 95

INTRODUCTION

Throughout history, no personality has commanded such profound authority and influence as our Lord and Savior, Jesus Christ. His victorious life and vicarious death continue to resonate across generations of mankind, transforming the lives and destinies of multitudes of people around the globe. Yet, it is in the unparalleled power of His resurrection that we find our ultimate identity, purpose and dominion, as His followers.

The resurrection stands as the defining moment of history. It was the moment that the foundation of our faith was laid and the floodgate of salvation, redemption, and eternal life was thrown open to all who would choose to embrace the risen Savior. Through the resurrection, Jesus not only conquered the grave but also ushered us into a new era of unprecedented move of God and restoration of our lost glory.

Nevertheless, there is still widespread ignorance, unbelief and levity in the attitude of many towards this phenomenal event. And, naturally, the manifold wonders and riches that flow from the resurrection continue to elude them. This unsettling reality propelled the inspiration for this book. Throughout the pages, you will find powerful revelations about the multifaceted dimensions and implications of the resurrection. You will uncover life-changing truths about the significance of the resurrection for humanity, in general, and for you, in particular.

With ample scriptural and real life proofs, you will discover how an encounter with the risen Savior will reposition your life, renew your faith, and reawaken you to a deeper sense of purpose. Essentially, this book is not merely a theological exploration but an invitation to encounter the triumphant Christ. It is a call to embrace the empowering reality of the resurrection power and allow it to permeate every aspect of your being, reflecting in your overall approach to life and eternity.

Whether you are a recent convert or seasoned believer seeking deeper spiritual insight, may the revelations in this book enrich your faith, ignite your spirit, and inspire you to live daily in the power of the risen Savior, Jesus Christ!

1
THE GREAT PROCLAMATION: HE IS RISEN!

Up from the grave He arose;
With a mighty triumph o'er his foes;
He arose a Victor from the dark domain,
And He lives forever, with His saints to reign.
He arose! He arose! Hallelujah! Christ arose!

– ROBERT LOWRY

It was just before dawn on Sunday morning, the third day after the death of Jesus Christ. The city of Jerusalem slumbered on in somber silence, still bearing the weight of the earth-shaking event. Particularly for His disciples and the multitudes of others who had been blessed by His life and ministry, the crucifixion had cast a pall of sorrow over them, leaving them baffled and grief-stricken. Yet, as the first light of day began to illuminate the horizon, a group of women who had faithfully followed Him, embarked on a solemn journey to His tomb.

Among them was Mary Magdalene, her heart heavy with sorrow, her steps faltering with each memory of the crucifixion. There were also Mary, the mother of James, and Salome, their hearts burdened by grief but their devotion unwavering. Carrying spices to anoint the body of their beloved Teacher, they made their way to the tomb, where Jesus had been laid to rest.

As they approached the tomb, their eyes strained against the darkness, searching for the massive stone that sealed its entrance and wondering how they would remove it. To their astonishment, they found the stone rolled away, and the entrance opened wide. Fear held them for a moment, as they wondered who could have done such a thing. Had the body of their Lord been stolen?

The women's hearts raced as they peered inside the tomb, but what they saw took their breath away.

There was no body there.

The burial linens were neatly folded and placed aside, as if the body they had come to anoint had simply disappeared.

"Where is He?" Mary Magdalene whispered, her voice trembling with emotion.

"He is not here," Mary, the mother of James, replied.

At that moment, their fear turned to confusion, and the confusion mingled with disbelief as they tried to make sense of the spectacle before them. Suddenly, two men in shining garments stood beside them, and their words echoed in the stillness of the morning: "WHY DO YOU SEEK THE LIVING AMONG THE DEAD? HE IS NOT HERE BUT IS RISEN!" And then they added, *"Remember how he told you, while he was still with you in Galilee: 'The Son of Man must be delivered over to the hands of sinners, be crucified and on the third day be raised again."*

With that remarkable proclamation and the recollection that Christ had indeed prophesied His death and resurrection, everything changed in that very moment. For the women, the dawn broke forth with a new light, as if the world itself recognized that something had happened that had never happened before. In that moment, the sunshine of hope shattered the darkness that had enveloped their souls. The realization that their Savior had indeed conquered death as He had promised filled them with a joy that surpassed all understanding.

As the women made their way back again through the streets of Jerusalem, their footsteps quickened with a newfound sense of hope and purpose. They had witnessed a spectacular miracle that would change the course of history forever. And thus, as the sun prophetically rose again over the city of Jerusalem, casting its golden light upon the land, the news of Jesus' resurrection began to spread, starting with His disciples.

Naturally, there were initial doubts and confusion; but these soon gave way to outbursts of triumphant praise, as the people of God realized that it was, indeed, a new dawn of hope, joy and assurance of life eternal for all believers in the risen Savior. The song in their heart and lips echoed that of the Psalmist in Psalm 126:1-3:

> *When the LORD restored the fortunes of Zion,*
> *we were like those who dreamed.*
> *Our mouths were filled with laughter,*
> *our tongues with songs of joy.*
> *Then it was said among the nations,*
> *"The LORD has done great things for them."*
> *The LORD has done great things for us,*
> *and we are filled with joy.*

My prayer for you, dear reader, is that, in this very season, there will be a sudden restoration of fortunes for you in all areas of your life. Every loss you have experienced shall be reversed and every trial shall become a testimony. By the power of the risen Christ, you will receive *"beauty for ashes, the oil of joy for mourning, the garment of praise for the spirit of heaviness"* (Isaiah 61:3, KJV)

A NEAR ANTI-CLIMAX

To fully appreciate the heights of joy that the disciples and other believers experienced following the news of Jesus' resurrection, you have to understand the depths of disappointment and dismay into which these same people had been plunged a few days before. The state of their mind is best captured in the lamentation of the two disciples on the way to Emmaus, *"And they said unto him, Concerning Jesus of Nazareth, which was a prophet mighty in deed and word before God and all the people: And how the chief priests and our rulers delivered him to be condemned to death, and have crucified him. But we trusted that it had been he which should have redeemed Israel..."* (Luke 24:19-21, KJV).

The truth, as the above verses reveal, is that there had been very great expectations of Jesus Christ because the people had thought so highly of Him. While some of these expectations (like those expressed on the way to Emmaus) had been misplaced, the fact remains that the life and ministry of Jesus had raised the hopes of the people so tremendously.

To provide context, His ministry had begun during one of the darkest periods in the history of the Jewish people. Not only were they politically oppressed by the dictatorial rule of the Roman authorities, but they were also heavily burdened by the religious excesses of the Pharisees and the Sadducees.

Thus, by His emancipating and empowering teaching of God's word (Mark 1:21-28), coupled with the diverse, unprecedented miracles He performed, most of the people had come to accept Jesus as the long-awaited Messiah. They had regarded Him as the "Anointed One" who had been sent to not only bring renewal to their faith and lead them back to God but also liberate them from the tyranny of the Roman Empire. So firm was their trust in Him and so desperate were they that they had actually considered forcefully making Him their king (John 6:15).

The disciples, in particular, had been so drawn to Jesus that they had forsaken all to follow Him. At a time, He had asked them if they would like to leave Him and their response was, *"Lord, to whom shall we go? You have the words of eternal life. We have come to believe and to know that you are the Holy One of God."* (John 6:68-69). At another time, He had inquired of them, *"Who do people say the Son of Man is?"* And they had replied, *"Some say John the Baptist; others say Elijah; and still others, Jeremiah or one of the prophets."* And He proceeded even further: *"But what about you?"* he asked. *"Who do you say I am?"* Simon Peter answered, *"You are the Messiah, the Son of the living God"* (Matthew 16:13-16).

This solid belief in Jesus' divinity and omnipotence had driven the disciples to vow to stand by Him at all cost, even if it meant losing their lives (Matthew 26:35). You can then imagine the extent of their confusion and hopelessness, when, right before their very eyes, the supposed deliverer had been captured and treated like a common criminal. And He had seemed powerless to defend or deliver Himself! Was He for real or had they been hoodwinked for so long by a fraud?

No wonder it did not take long for the disciples to desert him after His capture. Even Peter who had fiercely vowed to defend Him wasted no time in denying Him three times. In fact, on two of the occasions, he actually called Jesus "the man", with every sense of admiration gone! Such was the extent of their disappointment.

The crucifixion itself had been a public display of shame and ridicule, with Jesus hanging there helplessly, after being stripped, whipped, slapped, kicked, spat upon and terribly bruised. Those who had believed in Him might have still desperately clung to the last strands of hope, trusting that He could still perform a miracle – after all, he had delayed visiting Lazarus, until the latter was already dead.

But then, instead of the words of power and authority they had often heard from Him, what He uttered were anguished cries of thirst and being forsaken! Even when He was dared by the mocking mob to save Himself as He had saved others, He did absolutely nothing.

When He eventually died, the disciples did not only feel dejected and humiliated, they also became confused and distressed. They had lost hope and were uncertain about what the future held for them. Was this what they had staked the totality of their lives for?

No wonder a Bible commentary described Christ's death as the most shocking and hopeless event in history!

PERSONALIZED VIEW

Take a minute to personalize this experience, so you can get the picture even better. Put yourself in the shoes of the disciples. The man you had been following – the man you had believed to be God in the flesh - is now in the hands of the Roman authorities. At His public trial, you push through the throng to gain sight of your Savior, only to find Him bruised and battered.

The crowd screams at the one you love and adore, "Crucify Him!" Though no one can find fault in Him, the Roman governor (Pontius Pilate) caves in. He sentences Jesus to die, and Roman soldiers waste no time in whisking Him away. You follow as fast as you can.

You come upon the governor's headquarters. Pressing your ear to the walls, you hear the soldiers' insults. Peeking through a window, you see Jesus, utterly humiliated, standing in front of those He came to save. A crown of thorns sits atop His head and streams of blood pour down His face. Hit after hit, blow after blow, the Romans beat Him and shout, "Hail, king of the Jews!" (Mark 15:18).

Confusion rattles your mind. With your own eyes, you saw Jesus feed thousands with only a handful of bread and fish. You were there as He raised a dead man called Lazarus to life, and you watched him walk out of his tomb. You witnessed Jesus give blind men sight and lame men the ability to walk. Why is He just standing there?

Next, soldiers lead Him from the governor's headquarters to a hillside. They hang Him on a cross. As they nail His hands and feet to the wood, His screams of pain pierce your ears and break your heart. Naked and dying, Jesus speaks, as part of His final words, *"My God, my God, why have you forsaken me?"* (Mark 15:34). Soon after, He breathes His last breath. And to add to His humiliation, in order to prove that He is truly dead, one of the soldiers pierces His side with a spear, and immediately blood and water gush out (John 19:34).

Immediately, devastation overwhelms you. He was the One who was supposed to save you from death! He was the One who said He had brought life. You are hopeless, confused, and grief-stricken. Jesus has been killed. The one you considered God has died. Imagine this for a moment. Such monumental despair and hopelessness!

THE LAST LAUGH

But thanks be to God that neither the human enemies of Christ, nor the forces of darkness nor the grave could have the last say over Him. Just as He had foretold, Jesus conquered the fetters of death and arose from the tomb in power and majesty.

It was this victory that changed the reality of the disciples and that of multitudes of people around the world that would believe in His name. All of a sudden, for the disciples and other believers, fear and sadness changed to joy! Bad news changed to good news! Bleakness became brightness. Wretchedness became blessedness. Hopelessness turned to hopefulness, and the gloomy night turned to a glorious day!

Ultimately, the resurrection powerfully proves that whatever humanity has destroyed, Divinity can restore! I declare to you and your family right now, that your hope, joy and destiny are restored in Jesus' name!

2
PROOFS OF THE RESURRECTION

"I know of no one fact in the history of mankind which is proved by better and fuller evidence than the great sign which God hath given us - that Christ died and rose again from the dead".

– THOMAS ARNOLD

The renowned theologian and radio minister, John Vernon McGee, once received a letter from a lady who had listened to his radio program. The lady wrote: "Our teacher said that Jesus just swooned on the cross and that the disciples nursed him back to health. What do you think?"

Knowing that the so-called teacher must have been one of those peddling the "swoon theory", which states that Jesus did not really die at His crucifixion, but was merely unconscious when He was laid in the tomb and there He resuscitated, McGee gave an interesting reply. He said, *"Dear Sister, beat your teacher with a leather whip. Nail him to a cross. Hang him in the sun for six hours. Run a spear through his heart. Embalm him. Put him in an airless tomb for three days. Then see what happens."*

Indeed, the wonders and truths surrounding the resurrection of Jesus Christ are such that no one can deny without making a mockery of themselves. Let us quickly remind ourselves of three of these truths, not only to silence naysayers but more importantly to further strengthen our faith and better position us to fully enjoy the manifold blessings that the resurrection has brought to us.

1. THE EMPTY TOMB

The fact that the tomb of Jesus Christ was found empty is confirmed in all the four Gospels of the New Testament. The consistency across these multiple sources makes the resurrection undeniable. All those who visited the tomb, beginning with the women who had planned to anoint Christ's body, confirmed that they met an empty tomb. Interestingly, these same people had witnessed the brutal chain of events leading to His death and burial.

As to the certainty of the death itself, the Scripture leaves us in no doubt of the various measures taken to ensure that it was confirmed before the burial processes began. For instance, when the Jewish ruling council requested that the bodies of those crucified, including Jesus, be taken down from the cross because of the approach of the Sabbath day, the authorities had to first ensure that they were indeed dead.

John 19:31-34 narrates: *"Now it was the day of Preparation, and the next day was to be a special Sabbath. Because the Jewish leaders did not want the bodies left on the crosses during the Sabbath, they asked Pilate to have the legs broken and the bodies taken down. The soldiers therefore came and broke the legs of the first man who had been crucified with Jesus, and then those of the other. But when they came to Jesus and found that he was already dead, they did not break his legs. Instead, one of the soldiers pierced Jesus' side with a spear, bringing a sudden flow of blood and water."*

Again, when Joseph of Arimathea, who had witnessed the death of Jesus, came to ask for permission to bury His body, Pilate still had to double-check to avoid any error. According to Mark 15:42-45, "It was Preparation Day (that is, the day before the Sabbath). So as evening approached, Joseph of Arimathea, a prominent member of the Council, who was himself waiting for the kingdom of God, went boldly to Pilate and asked for Jesus' body. Pilate was surprised to hear that he was already dead. Summoning the centurion, he asked him if Jesus had already died. When he learned from the centurion that it was so, he gave the body to Joseph." That effectively rubbishes the swoon theory and other baseless fabrications.

As hinted above, some of those who witnessed the death of Jesus also witnessed His burial. Luke 23:55-56 says, for example, *"The women who had come with Jesus from Galilee followed Joseph and saw the tomb and how his body was laid in it. Then they went home and prepared spices and perfumes. But they rested on the Sabbath in obedience to the commandment."*

The women had to follow Joseph, so they could know the exact tomb in which Jesus would be laid. This was in anticipation of the embalmment, which they wanted to carry out on Him after the Sabbath. In essence, what they were expecting to see on Sunday, was a corpse in the early stages of decomposition. What they found however was a mind-boggling and life-changing miracle.

My prayer for you today is that those who knew you before and expected nothing good to come out of will be shocked by your miraculous turnaround in Jesus name!

To further understand how significant this empty tomb miracle is, you should recall the painstaking efforts made by the authorities to safeguard the tomb from being accessed by any intruder or "deceiver", as the jittery authorities termed it. "The next day, the one after Preparation Day, the chief priests and the Pharisees went to Pilate. "Sir," they said, "we remember that while he was still alive that deceiver said, 'After three days I will rise again.' So give the order for the tomb to be made secure until the third day. Otherwise, his disciples may come and steal the body and tell the people that he has been raised from the dead. This last deception will be worse than the first." "Take a guard," Pilate answered. *"Go, make the tomb as secure as you know how." So they went and made the tomb secure by putting a seal on the stone and posting the guard."* (Matthew 27:62-66).

What I want you to note here, first of all, is that the religious leaders only requested for a three-day watch over the tomb, being mindful that Jesus had said he would resurrect on the third day. This means that they were absolutely sure of His being dead, as well as what they considered the impossibility of His resurrecting. What they were anxious about was the possibility of someone gaining access to His body within the three days, and claiming that He had indeed resurrected. So, they did all they could to keep the tomb inaccessible to any human.

But the Almighty God shocked them in ways they could never have imagined. *"There was a violent earthquake, for an angel of the Lord came down from heaven and, going to the tomb, rolled back the stone and sat on it. His appearance was like lightning, and his clothes were white as snow. The guards were so afraid of him that they shook and became like dead men."* (Matthew 28:2-4). Halleluiah!

By the way, let me remind you that while the women who would eventually be the first to witness the resurrection were still on their way to the tomb, the huge stone at the mouth of the tomb was a major concern to them. They kept wondering, *"Who will roll the stone away from the entrance of the tomb?"* (Mark (16:3). But, guess what? That did not stop them from going ahead with their mission. They stepped out in faith and the resurrection power of the Almighty God came to their rescue. *"But when they looked up, they saw that the stone, which was very large, had been rolled away"* (Mark 16:4). Glory to God!

I challenge you today that whatever it is that you have been inspired to achieve, move towards it by faith, not minding the foreseeable or forecasted challenges. I assure you that by the time you get there, every stone of difficulty would have been rolled away, in the mighty name of Jesus. I declare into your life that, by the power of the resurrection, any stone that is preventing the accomplishment of God's plan and purpose for your life, the Lord will remove and sit on it, in the mighty name of Jesus. And you will walk straight into the purpose and program that God has for you, in the name of Jesus.

I declare into your life that the power of God will undo every damage the enemy has wreaked upon you and your household. Every stronghold of limitation and every yoke that is meant to keep you down is uprooted today, in the name of Jesus.

Still on the empty tomb, it will interest you to note that even the Jewish authorities and the Roman soldiers assigned to guard the body acknowledged this truth. According to Matthew 28:11-15, *"While the women were on their way, some of the guards went into the city and reported to the chief priests everything that had happened. When the chief priests had met with the elders and devised a plan, they gave the soldiers a large sum of money, telling them, "You are to say, 'His disciples came during the night and stole him away while we were asleep.' If this report gets to the governor, we will satisfy him and keep you out of trouble." So the soldiers took the money and did as they were instructed. And this story has been widely circulated among the Jews to this very day."*

In bribing the soldiers to spread a false story about the theft of Jesus' body, the Jewish leaders implicitly confirmed that the tomb was indeed empty!

2. POST-RESURRECTION APPEARANCES

Soon after His resurrection, Jesus showed Himself in person to His followers at different times within a period of 40 days. And you know what? None of those who saw Him ever remained the same again. Acts 1:3 narrates that *"after his suffering, he presented himself to them and gave many convincing proofs that he was alive. He appeared to them over a period of forty days and spoke about the kingdom of God."*

I need to quickly call your attention to something here. As we will see shortly, most of the people that the risen Christ appeared to were people you would never have expected Him to appear to – from women who were considered inadequate, to men who had denied Him and doubted His divinity and resurrection. Of course, as the strategic Master that He is, Jesus did not appear to these people merely for the sake of showmanship; rather, He did so to accomplish specific purposes in their lives. And I believe that He will accomplish even much more in your life. So, don't write yourself off or see yourself as being too vile to be visited and impacted by the resurrected Christ. If you would invite Him into your life today and make Him your Savior and Lord, He will make something awesome out of your life!

Interestingly also, many of those whom the risen Christ appeared to did not initially recognize Him – despite having accompanied Him throughout His ministry. The same still happens today. Many attend church programs and seem very close to ministers of God but they never seem to see God. I pray for you today that may God reveal Himself to you in this season. And may every scale that prevents you from seeing Jesus in your life in every situation, be removed by the resurrection power.

Before giving an overview of the reasons for the post-resurrection appearances, let us briefly examine some of instances of the appearances.

- **Mary Magdalene**

Mary Magdalene was the first to see the resurrected Jesus. Yes – the same Mary Magdalene from whom He had once cast out seven demons! (Luke 8:2). According to John 20:11-18, she encountered Him outside the tomb and initially mistook Him for the gardener until He revealed Himself to her by calling her name. Apparently, there was something about the way the Lord called "Mary" that she knew nobody else could. And, casting off the veil of gloom and despair that had enveloped her, she blurted out with unspeakable joy, "Rabboni!" (which means "Teacher"). (John 20:16).

Rest assured, reader, that the Lord knows your name and He will call and speak to you in a way that will reach the deepest part of your soul and banish your fears and doubts. I pray that you have the same encounter with Him as Mary Magdalene did!

One major factor that enabled Mary Magdalene to be the first to see the Savior was her persistence. According John's Gospel, when Mary saw the empty tomb, her first reaction was to run back to the disciples to report the situation to them. Mary Magdalene came to the tomb and found it empty and went to tell the disciples. This prompted Peter and John to rush to the tomb. And you know what? Mary also went back to the tomb with them; and even after the disciples had confirmed that it was empty and left, she stayed back crying. Then, she decided to peer into the tomb once more and that was when she saw two angles seated inside. And shortly after, she turned and saw the risen Lord Himself!

What does this tell you? If you persistently seek Jesus, He will reveal Himself to you - whether it is to know Him more (Philippians 3:10) or to have a problem solved. Indeed, God has promised that *"you will seek me and find me when you seek me with all your heart"* (Jeremiah 29:13).

- **The Disciples on the Road To Emmaus**

Two of Jesus' disciples were walking to the village of Emmaus when Jesus appeared to them, although they did not recognize him at first. They talked with him about recent events, and it was only when he broke bread with them that they realized it was Jesus (Luke

24:13-35).

Again, what was special about breaking bread that eventually opened their eyes? It was the unmistakable way in which the Savior did it. You cannot have a real encounter with Christ and not be impacted!

And the sweetest part was the testimony the disciples gave about the way Jesus spoke to them. Just like Mary, there was a powerful stirring in their spirit. According to them, *"Were not our hearts burning within us while he talked with us on the road and opened the Scriptures to us?"* (Luke 24:32). I declare again that the right encounter and word you need to transform your life and destiny will be dropped into your spirit today by the power of the risen Christ!

- **The Disciples in the Upper Room**

According to Luke 24:36-49 and John 20:19-23, Jesus appeared to His disciples in a locked room in Jerusalem. He showed them His hands and feet, proving He was not a ghost but truly resurrected. As with the other people who encountered the risen Christ, the disciples were not left untouched. John 20:20-22 says, *"The disciples were overjoyed when they saw the Lord. Again Jesus said, 'Peace be with you! As the Father has sent me, I am sending you.' And with that he breathed on them and said, "Receive the*

Holy Spirit."

Every visitation from the Lord comes with an unforgettable impartation. Seek Him and you will receive yours!

- **Thomas**

What a considerate and compassionate Savior we have! As the Scripture clearly reveal, when the risen Lord appeared to the disciples in the Upper Room, Thomas was not present. He consequently continued to doubt the resurrection. Therefore, Jesus had to schedule another visitation for Thomas exactly a week later, inviting him to touch His scars!

Well, as you would expect, that experience had a transformative effect on Thomas. If the woman with the issue of blood who merely touched the helm of Jesus' garment could be delivered of her yoke, you can imagine the impact of Thomas' touching the very scars on Jesus' body. The walls of doubts and unbelief were immediately broken down and Thomas proclaimed, "My Lord and my God!" (John 20:24-29).

As you encounter the Savior this moment, every stronghold resisting the move of God in your life is broken down, in Jesus' name!

- **Peter and Other Disciples**

Just as our loving Savior did with Thomas, dealing with Him according to the peculiarity of his spiritual and psychological condition, He also did same with Peter. In actual fact, His special consideration for Peter began to manifest immediately after the resurrection. Knowing how devastated and embarrassed Peter must have been for repeatedly denying Him, the risen Christ sent him a special message through the angel at the tomb. "Don't be alarmed," he said. *"You are looking for Jesus the Nazarene, who was crucified. He has risen! He is not here. See the place where they laid him. But go, tell his disciples and Peter, 'He is going ahead of you into Galilee. There you will see him, just as he told you.'"* (Mark 16:6-7).

Jesus singled out Peter's name to reassure him of His undying love and forgiveness. However, despite the message, Peter still seemed to feel dejected and unworthy to continue as a disciple. He thought that it was the end of the road for him and all the wonderful promises that Christ had made concerning His destiny. So discouraged was he that he had to tell the other disciples that he was returning to his former trade. But just in the nick of time, the risen Christ appeared to restore Peter and reawaken the zeal for God in him (See John 21:1-19).

Interestingly, as with the other instances of Christ's post-resurrection appearances, this particular encounter came with showers of blessings for the disciples. *"Afterward Jesus appeared again to his disciples, by the Sea of Galilee. It happened this way: Simon Peter, Thomas (also known as Didymus), Nathanael from Cana in Galilee, the sons of Zebedee, and two other disciples were together. "I'm going out to fish," Simon Peter told them, and they said, "We'll go with you."* So they went out and got into the boat, but that night they caught nothing. Early in the morning, Jesus stood on the shore, but the disciples did not realize that it was Jesus. He called out to them, *"Friends, haven't you any fish?" "No," they answered. He said, "Throw your net on the right side of the boat and you will find some."* When they did, they were unable to haul the net in because of the large number of fish. Then the disciple whom Jesus loved said to Peter, *"It is the Lord..."* (John 21:1-7).

You see what happened there? How did the Lord make them realize His identity? By instantly turning their failure to success. Remember what we established earlier? Every visitation from the Lord must come with an unforgettable impartation in your life. I decree this moment that you will have that encounter with the risen

Savior that will turn all the failures, disappointments and miseries of your life to breakthroughs and testimonies, in the name of Jesus.

- **The Ascension**

The last appearance of Jesus recorded in the Bible is His ascension to heaven. Forty days after his resurrection, Jesus led his disciples to the Mount of Olives. As other times, He ensured to bless their lives before ascending into heaven in their presence (Luke 24:50-53, Acts 1:6-11).

In all, Apostle Paul specifically mentions that the risen Christ appeared to more 500 people, including those who had not been His followers. Prominent among these were James (His brother) and Paull Himself! According to Paul, "For what I received I passed on to you as of first importance: that Christ died for our sins according to the Scriptures, that he was buried, that he was raised on the third day according to the Scriptures, and that he appeared to Cephas, and then to the Twelve. After that, he appeared to more than five hundred of the brothers and sisters at the same time, most of whom are still living, though some have fallen asleep. Then he appeared to James, then to all the apostles, and last of all he appeared to me also, as to one abnormally born.

For I am the least of the apostles and do not even deserve to be called an apostle, because I persecuted the church of God" (1 Corinthians 15:3-9).

We will dwell more on the above experience of Paul in the next point.

- **The Disciples' Transformation**

This, perhaps, is the most undeniable proof of the resurrection. The change in character, courage and conviction that came upon the disciples and all who claimed to have encountered the risen Christ was, to say the least, phenomenal! It was such that cannot be explained by any other means than the fact that they saw and experienced something so unforgettable and undisputable.

Let us begin with the disciples. What made their transformation so wonderful and so surreal is that even they had not expected the resurrection to happen. This was what made them to become so dejected after His death. When the women, in their sorrowful state, went to His tomb and could not find His body, it never occurred to them that He could have risen. It was when the angels told them, "He is not here; he has risen! Remember how he told you, while he was still with you in Galilee: 'The Son of Man must be delivered over to the hands of sinners, be crucified and on the third day be raised again" that "they remembered his words." (Luke 24:6-8).

Again, when the women rushed back to deliver the good news to the disciples, where they were huddled up in fear and despair, the Bible records that "they did not believe the women, because their words seemed to them like nonsense." (Luke 24:11).

Now, fast-forward to that book of the Bible that contains so many missionary exploits done by the same followers of Jesus that it was named *"The Acts of the Apostles"* and tell me what happened in-between. It was the impact of the risen Christ that they saw! As J.C. Ryle, first Anglican bishop of Liverpool, wrote: *"The unbelief of the apostles is one of the strongest indirect evidences that Jesus rose from the dead. If the disciples were at first so backward to believe our Lord's resurrection, and were at last so thoroughly persuaded of its truth, that they preached it everywhere — then Christ must have risen indeed."*

That the disciples frequently and fearlessly preached about the resurrection is in no doubt, and Peter is a good example here. As we saw earlier, not only did he, just like other disciples, forsake Jesus out of fear but he actually lost his spiritual fervor after Jesus' death. However following the post-resurrection encounters with Jesus, he became a totally different person, with all his fears and doubts gone. As people gathered to watch and mock them because they spoke in tongues on the day of Pentecost, it was Peter who boldly led the others to declare: *"Fellow Israelites, listen to this: Jesus of Nazareth was a man accredited by God to you by miracles, wonders and signs, which God did among you through him, as you yourselves know. This man was handed over to you by God's deliberate plan and foreknowledge; and you, with the help of wicked men, put him to death by nailing him to the cross. But God raised him from the dead, freeing him from the agony of death, because it was impossible for death to keep its hold on him…"* (Acts 2:22-24).

How did a man, who timidly cowered before a maid and blatantly denied ever meeting Jesus, suddenly become the staunchest and fiercest defender of His ministry, death and resurrection? I am sure you already know the answer!

And guess what? This same unshakeable and unstoppable boldness was manifested by other disciples and believers in Christ throughout their lifetimes. In fact, the majority of them chose to be battered, stoned, drowned, hung or beheaded, while clinging to their faith and testimony of the resurrection.

Here is how someone put it: *"The Apostles went through a dramatic change. Within a few weeks, they were standing face to face with the ones who had crucified their leader. Their spirit was like iron. They became unstoppable in their determination to sacrifice everything for the one they called Savior and Lord. Even after they were imprisoned, threatened, and forbidden to speak in the name of Jesus, the apostles said to the Jewish leaders, "We ought to obey God rather than men"* (Acts 5:29)!

Overall, the above irrefutable proofs of Jesus' resurrection provide a message of hope, courage, and purpose for all Christians. It reminds us that God is with us, and that His promises are true and trustworthy. It inspires us to live our lives with unconquerable faith, hope, and assurance, knowing that we are children of the risen and reigning Christ!

3
CRUCIFIXION: THE BEGINNING OF RESURRECTION BLESSINGS

"By His death on the Cross, Christ has become the Lamb that was slain for us, our Redeemer, the One who has made peace between us and God, who has taken our guilt on Himself, who has conquered our most deadly enemy and has assuaged the well-deserved wrath of God."

- MARK DEVER

So manifold and multi-dimensional are the blessings that came with the resurrection, and we will be diving into them shortly. However, we cannot fully understand what happened at the resurrection of Christ, without rewinding back to His crucifixion and death. This is not just because there cannot be a resurrection without a death but more importantly because, in the case of Christ, the blessings of the resurrection are actually the culmination of the blessings that began with the crucifixion. Simply put, to fully understand and enjoy the blessings that came with the resurrection, we must begin with the wonders that came with the crucifixion.

Apparently, it was ignorance of this truth that made the disciples of Jesus Christ to be so heartbroken about His death. Based on their understanding and experience, death was a dreadful enemy that implied the cessation of life and termination of hope. They loved Jesus being physically around but did not understand that He was not born to live but to die, so that the entire human race could live again. He actually gave them this hint prior to His crucifixion, saying: *"Very truly I tell you, unless a kernel of wheat falls to the ground and dies, it remains only a single seed. But if it dies, it produces many seeds"* (John 12:24).

You can then understand why He was so blunt in His reply to the two disciples on the road to Emmaus, who were lamenting His death. He sounded really unimpressed as He told them, *"How foolish you are, and how slow to believe all that the prophets have spoken! Did not the Messiah have to suffer these things and then enter his glory?"* (Luke 24:25-26).

PAINFUL NECESSITY

Jesus made it clear to the disciples that His death was not a calamity but a necessity. The reasons for this necessity are what we are examining in this chapter. Bear in mind, however, that Jesus' speaking so positively about His suffering and death does not mean that it was an easy or enjoyable experience for Him. On the contrary, it was the most excruciating and humiliating experience that you can imagine.

The ancient Romans reserved death by crucifixion for those considered to be the worst of criminals and therefore deserving the worst of torture and humiliation possible. As Greg Gilbert explains, *"Shredded flesh against unforgiving wood, iron stakes pounded through bone and wracked nerves, joints wrenched out of socket by the sheer dead weight of the body, public humiliation before the eyes of family, friends, and the world – that was death on the cross."*

In fact, so horrible was death by crucifixion that even the thought of it made Jesus wish it could be avoided; but His love for mankind and submission to the Divine will made Him to go through it. Here is how Matthew 26:36-39 narrates this: *"Then Jesus went with his disciples to a place called Gethsemane, and he said to them, "Sit here while I go over there and pray."* He took Peter and the two sons of Zebedee along with him, and he began to be sorrowful and troubled. Then he said to them, *"My soul is overwhelmed with sorrow to the point of death. Stay here and keep watch with me."* Going a little farther, he fell with his face to the ground and prayed, *"My*

Father, if it is possible, may this cup be taken from me. Yet not as I will, but as you will."

You will understand better why Jesus was in such a sorrowful state when you realize the extent of physical and psychological agony He had to endure by choosing to die on the cross. The late preacher, Frederick Farrar, gave this detailed description:

A death by crucifixion seems to include all that pain and death can have of the horrible and ghastly – dizziness, cramp, thirst, starvation, sleeplessness, traumatic fever, shame, publicity of shame, long continuous torment, horror of anticipation, mortification of intended wounds – all intensified just up to the point at which they can be endured at all, but all stopping just short of the point which would give to the sufferer the relief of unconsciousness.

The unnatural position made every movement painful; the lacerated veins and crushed tendons throbbed with incessant anguish; the wounds, inflamed by exposure, gradually gangrene; the arteries – especially at the head and stomach – became swollen and oppressed with surcharged blood, and while each variety of misery went on gradually increasing, there was added to them the intolerable pang of a burning and raging thirst, and all these physical complications caused an internal excitement and anxiety, which made the prospect of death itself – of death, the unknown enemy, at whose approach man usually shudders most – bear the aspect of a delicious and exquisite release.

What an experience! My earnest prayer is that the suffering and death of Christ will not be in vain in your life.

PROMISED REDEEMER

So, the question again is, why did Christ have to endure such a horror that was meant to inflict maximum pain and shame? The answer lies in the fall of man in Eden and the provision for redemption that God immediately made for mankind. In Genesis 3:15, God told the devil, represented by the serpent, *"And I will put enmity between you and the woman, and between your offspring and hers; he will crush your head, and you will strike his heel."*

In warfare, striking the heel signifies a minor, temporary blow; while crushing the head signifies a fatal and permanent defeat. In the context of our passage, the head of the serpent is its strength and the armory for its deadly poison. Thus, the crushing of its head represents irreversible defeat. The "offspring" of the woman here is prophetic about Jesus, who would endure some bruising from the offspring of the serpent, so He could gain total victory over the serpent and liberate mankind. As 1 John 3:8 says, *"The reason the Son of God appeared was to destroy the devil's work."*

I believe you already know how mankind fell into the captivity of the devil through disobedience; but beyond the fall are the grave and lasting implications. For starters, by that singular disobedience to God and yielding to the deceiver, mankind became spiritually separated from God and sold under the cruel dominion of the devil. Consequently mankind became not only slaves to the power of sin but also afflictions, oppressions, sicknesses, diseases, crises and any other misfortune you can think of. This is why Jesus said, *"The thief comes only to steal and kill and destroy; I have come that they may have life, and have it to the full"* (John 10:10).

Basically, it was for us to regain life without limitations that Christ came to suffer and die. As John Piper aptly explained, *"God is not content to leave all people under His wrath. Nor can he simply sweep sin under the rug of the universe. Therefore His love and His justice conspire to make a way for sinners to be saved and God's justice to be vindicated. The answer is the death of Jesus Christ."*

Prophet Isaiah gave a graphic picture of the extent Jesus went for our redemption, saying: *"He was despised and rejected by mankind, a man of suffering, and familiar with pain. Like one from whom people hide their faces he was despised, and we held him in low esteem. Surely he took up our pain and bore our suffering, yet we considered him punished by God, stricken by him, and afflicted. But he was pierced for our transgressions, he was crushed for our iniquities; the punishment that brought us peace was on him, and by his wounds we are healed. We all, like sheep, have gone astray, each of us has turned to our own way; and the LORD has laid on him the iniquity of us all. He was oppressed and afflicted, yet he did not open his mouth; he was led like a lamb to the slaughter, and as a sheep before its shearers is silent, so he did not open his mouth."* (Isaiah 53:3-7).

BUT WHY JESUS CHRIST?

This is an aspect of this whole mystery of redemption that may still be gnawing at your mind. Why did God have to send *"His only begotten Son"* (John 3:16) to die for mankind? Why could not another human do it? Here is the answer: No man could have been able to do it because all mankind was under the captivity and curse of sin. *"For all have sinned and fall short of the glory of God"* (Romans 3:23).

Recall that God had clearly warned the first man, Adam, *"You are free to eat from any tree in the garden; but you must not eat from the tree of the knowledge of good and evil, for when you eat from it you will certainly die"* (Genesis 2:16-17). It was as if God was giving man the opportunity of obeying Him and living eternally or disobeying and dying eternally.

Well, since man chose to disobey, death (representing loss of the divine nature and other privileges) naturally followed, and thereby affecting his offspring and mankind, in general. That automatically imposes a limitation and makes every natural man incapable of rescuing himself, much less the rest of humanity. As Romans 5:12-14 says, *"When Adam sinned, sin entered the world. Adam's sin brought death, so death spread to everyone, for everyone sinned. Yes…everyone died—from the time of Adam to the time of Moses—even those who did not disobey an explicit commandment of God, as Adam did"* (NLT).

It follows then that if man must be redeemed and restored, the perfect price for sin must be paid for the holy and just God to be appeased and the curse attached to the fall to be removed. But which man was qualified to do this, with all mankind being in the same sinful and helpless state? This was where the sinless Son of God, Jesus Christ, had to come in.

Anselm of Canterbury, the outstanding theologian of the 11th century, shed some light on this: *"It would not have been right for the restoration of human nature to be left undone, and it could not have been done unless man paid what was owing to God for sin. But the debt was so great that, while man alone owed it, only God could pay it, so that the same person must be both man and God."* J.C. Ryle also adds, *"The death of Christ was necessary to our salvation. Without the death of Christ, God's law could never have been satisfied, sin could never have been pardoned, man could never have been justified before God, and God could never have shown mercy to man."*

In essence, Jesus had to come and die because God, in His infinite holiness and justice, required a proportionate penalty for man's sin; but in His infinite compassion and love, He provided the perfect sacrifice that man was too powerless and unworthy to provide. What an awesome God we serve!

4
THE WONDERS OF CHRIST'S DEATH

"Come, and see the victories of the cross. Christ's wounds are thy healings, His agonies thy repose, His conflicts thy conquests, His groans thy songs, His pains thine ease, His shame thy glory, His death thy life, His sufferings thy salvation.

- MATTHEW HENRY

So, now that we understand what led to Christ's death before His eventual resurrection, what specific blessings were released to us by such cruel suffering and death?

1. ATONEMENT AND REMOVAL OF SIN

Right there on the cross, all our sins were simply transferred to Jesus Christ. He took our place as the one who had offended God, while His own righteousness was transferred to us. As 2 Corinthians 5:21 says, *"God made him who had no sin to be sin for us, so that in him we might become the righteousness of God."*

In other words, Christ's death satisfied the demands of divine justice and totally cleared our enormous sin-debt to God. Therefore, whoever comes to God today in repentance, regardless of how many or monstrous their sin-burden may be, Christ has paid for it all; and God will, by Christ's sacrifice, forgive and transfer His righteousness to them. This is what Isaiah meant when He said, *"the LORD has laid on him the iniquity of us all."*

To better understand how Jesus accomplished the work of bearing away the sins of humanity, simply cast your mind back to the scapegoat used on the Day of Atonement in the Old Testament. Leviticus 16:20-22 says, *"When Aaron has finished making atonement for the Most Holy Place, the tent of meeting and the altar, he shall bring forward the live goat. He is to lay both hands on the head of the live goat and confess over it all the wickedness and rebellion of the Israelites—all their sins—and put them on the goat's head. He shall send the goat away into the wilderness in the care of someone appointed for the task. The goat will carry on itself all their sins to a remote place; and the man shall release it in the wilderness."*

Now, since Jesus compassionately chose to bear the entire iniquity of humanity on Himself, He automatically also bore the heavy punishment that came with sin, thereby assuaging God's wrath. He simply absorbed God's wrath against all of mankind in His own person. This was why He had to endure so much agony and shame. As we have seen earlier, the cost of sin is great and deadly. However, the reason we can simply confess our sins to God and receive instant forgiveness is because Christ paid the penalty for sin on our behalf.

2. RECONCILIATION WITH GOD

One of the greatest wonders of the cross is reconciliation with God and restoration of our place as God's special creation. 1 Peter 2:9-10 says, *"But you are a chosen people, a royal priesthood, a holy nation, God's special possession, that you may declare the praises of him who called you out of darkness into his wonderful light. Once you were not a people, but now you are the people of God; once you had not received mercy, but now you have received mercy."*

How did this become possible? 1 Timothy 2:5-6 has the answer! *"For there is one God and one mediator between God and mankind, the man Christ Jesus, who gave himself as a ransom for all people."*

By His death on the cross, Jesus has made Himself the ransom and peacemaker between God and man. Therefore, the moment we come to God in repentance, while appropriating the death of Christ, we are justified before God and seen as having never sinned. We become entirely new creation. As 2 Corinthians 5:17-19 says, *"Therefore, if anyone is in Christ, he is a new creation; old things have passed away; behold, all things have become new. Now all things are of*

God, who has reconciled us to Himself through Jesus Christ, and has given us the ministry of reconciliation, that is, that God was in Christ reconciling the world to Himself, not imputing their trespasses to them…"

With this reconciliation, we immediately receive the life of God in us and automatically gain access to the treasures of His Kingdom.

3. POWER FOR RIGHTEOUSNESS

Before Christ came to offer himself on the cross, there were temporary measures in place for the atonement of sin. We saw an example above of the scapegoat. There were other provisions, such as burnt offerings and the use of the blood of lambs, bulls and goats. However, these had their limitations - the biggest of which is that, while the blood from these animals helped an individual to obtain mercy from God, they could not deliver the individual from the captivity of sin. Not even the priests who helped the people to make atonement had the power to live the righteous life that God's holiness demands. It was a daily struggle to live in obedience to God's word.

But glory be to God that Jesus offered His own blood for atonement and the breaking of the yoke of sin, once and for all. Righteousness has now become a lifestyle, rather than a stressful obligation. Halleluiah! Hebrews 10:4-14 affirms this: *"It is impossible for the blood of bulls and goats to take away sins. Therefore, when Christ came into the world, he said: "Sacrifice and offering you did not desire, but a body you prepared for me; with burnt offerings and sin offerings you were not pleased. Then I said, 'Here I am—it is written about me in the scroll —I have come to do your will, my God…' Day after day every priest stands and performs his religious duties; again and again he offers the same sacrifices, which can never take away sins. But when this priest had offered for all time one sacrifice for sins, he sat down at the right hand of God, and since that time he waits for his enemies to be made his footstool. For by one sacrifice he has made perfect forever those who are being made holy."*

Now you see why Jesus had to die – His precious blood needed to be shed, so that you and I can be sanctified (made holy) and empowered to live in righteousness all the days of our lives. What this means is that there is no sinful habit or addiction that you cannot overcome through the purifying and grace-imparting blood of Jesus. *'For sin shall no longer be your master, because you are not under the law, but under grace* (Romans 6:14). Praise God!

4. HEALING AND DELIVERANCE

Another glorious blessing of the cross is the procurement of healing and deliverance for humanity. To put it simply, the reason Jesus' body was battered was so that our bodies could be bettered – with every cell, tissue and organ functioning optimally and fortified against sicknesses and diseases. Here again is Isaiah 53:5, *"But he was wounded for our transgressions, he was bruised for our iniquities: the chastisement of our peace was upon him; and with his stripes we are healed"* (KJV).

Bear in mind that the healing and health procured by Christ through His suffering and death is a holistic one. This means that it is not just effective against the infirmities of the body but also those of the soul and spirit. The World Health Organization defines health as a state of "complete physical, mental and social well-being and not merely the absence of disease or infirmity." This and many more are what the bruised body of Jesus and His precious blood have obtained for us.

As a proof of this, Matthew 8:16-17, in reference to Christ's ministry, says, *"When evening came, many who were demon-possessed were brought to him, and he drove out the spirits with a word and healed all the sick. This was to fulfill what was spoken through the prophet Isaiah: "He took up our infirmities and bore our diseases.""*

The fact that Jesus healed not only those who had sicknesses but also those afflicted by evil spirits shows that the healing provision we have in God through Jesus' death is a total one. Especially, in these days, when more and more people are having mental health crisis, there is assured relief and succor in the stripes and blood of Jesus.

Indeed, the blood of Jesus is the greatest immunity and cure for any kind of disease or sickness you can think of. Immerse yourself daily in the pool of this blood and you will have no need to fear *"the terror of night, nor the arrow that flies by day, nor the pestilence that stalks in the darkness, nor the plague that destroys at midday"* (Psalms 91:5-6).

5. DOMINION AND ALL-ROUND PROVISION

The death of Christ has paid the price for us to be restored to the place of power and dominion that we were created to function in at the beginning. In this privileged place, there is no fear, weakness, failure or limitation. It is life and life in abundance (John 10:10).

Moreover, this exalted place has immunity against every curse – personal or generational – as the Scriptures says, *"Christ has redeemed us from the curse of the law, having become a curse for us (for it is written, "Cursed is everyone who hangs on a tree"), that the blessing of Abraham might come upon the Gentiles in Christ Jesus, that we might receive the promise of the Spirit through faith."* (Galatians 3:13-14).

Most importantly, the death of Christ on the cross is the most compelling demonstration of the depth of God's love for mankind and the extent to which He can go to ensure that we have all we need to enjoy life on earth and live with

Him ultimately. As Romans 8:32 reveals, *"He who did not spare his own Son, but gave him up for us all—how will he not also, along with him, graciously give us all things?"* (Romans 8:32).

Therefore, through the sacrificial death of Jesus Christ, you are entitled to the best provisions of God's Kingdom. And guess what? This includes even financial prosperity! *"For you know the grace of our Lord Jesus Christ, that though he was rich, yet for your sake he became poor, so that you through his poverty might become rich"* (2 Corinthians 8:9). No more financial struggles for you, in the name of Jesus!

FORESHADOWS OF THE RESURRECTION POWER

Now that we have dwelt extensively on the purpose and wonders of Christ's death, we need to ask: What happened between the time of His death and resurrection? Was the Great Redeemer simply lying there – cold, limp and undergoing the early stages of decomposition like every other human? Science tells us that the internal organs of a dead body begin to decompose between 24 and 72 hours after death. Was the Messiah also subjected to such degradation?

Definitely not. Psalm 16:10 says, *"For you will not leave my soul among the dead or allow your holy one to rot in the grave"* (NLT). Even in death, the unstoppable Messiah continued

His mission of perfecting the liberation of mankind. Remember that before He died, He had predicted that His case would be like that of Jonah being swallowed by the whale (Matthew 12:40). Now, was Jonah lying limp in the belly of the fish? Not at all. The Scripture records that *"Now the LORD provided a huge fish to swallow Jonah, and Jonah was in the belly of the fish three days and three nights. From inside the fish Jonah prayed to the LORD his God..."* (Jonah 1:17 - 2:1).

Now that you have some idea, let us have a closer look at the events in that critical interval of death and resurrection. To begin with, so glorious and victorious was Christ in death that the centurion at the foot of His cross and other soldiers with him exclaimed, *"Surely he was the Son of God!"* (Matthew 27:54). What prompted this reaction? The preceding verses tell us that immediately Jesus died, *"the curtain of the temple was torn in two from top to bottom. The earth shook, the rocks split and the tombs broke open. The bodies of many holy people who had died were raised to life..."* (Matthew 27:51-52). Halleluiah!

Understand that those accompanying incidents were not mere theatrics or coincidences; they were demonstrations and foretastes of the blessings that are ours through Christ's death and subsequent resurrection. First, the tearing of the curtain symbolizes the opening of access to God. Until that unprecedented sacrifice that Jesus made on the cross, the temple had a curtain (veil) that separated the Holy of

Holies, where the presence of God dwelled, from the rest of the structure. Simply put, the curtain served to separate people from the direct presence of God.

Nobody was permitted to look into, much less enter into the special place. Even the high priest could only enter it once a year, on the great day of atonement. But to do so, he must have the blood of atonement in his hands, which he sprinkled upon and before the mercy seat seven times (Leviticus 16:14). However, following the completion of His sacrifice on the cross, Jesus made what was impossible to become possible. The veil that had hindered generations of people from enjoying the blessings of the presence and glory of God was ripped in two, from top to bottom (representing totality).

As a result, we now have the liberty to *"approach God's throne of grace with confidence, so that we may receive mercy and find grace to help us in our time of need"* (Hebrews 4:16). I decree into your life that, from today, every impossibility of your life shall become possible. And every veil that has prevented you from enjoying the fullness of God's glory shall be completely destroyed, in the name of Jesus!

The second event was that "the earth shook" (earthquake). This was to literally demonstrate the earth-shaking impact that the death and resurrection would have on the world and, indeed, every aspect of creation. It was to demonstrate that the world would no longer be the same again. It was the beginning of a new dawn, a new order, in worship and other aspects of life.

Interestingly, years later, as the apostle began to powerfully witness to the resurrection power, people actually testified that they had successfully "turned the world upside down" (Acts 17:6, KJV). I pray for you that, by the power of the risen Christ in you, you are the next person to cause a positive transformation in your world!

The third event was that the rocks split. Even before His resurrection, the power of the unstoppable Christ was already demonstrating that the world was in the process of experiencing the most historic moment in its history. Rocks represent seemingly immoveable strongholds and longstanding impediments. By His death, however, the Lord Jesus dismantled those strongholds and proved that no mountain, predicament, dilemma or crisis will be too difficult for anyone carrying the power of the risen Christ.

I decree that your destiny shall begin to experience an unprecedented shift from this moment. Every longstanding challenge, difficulty, limitation, curse or infirmity is uprooted from your life, in Jesus' name.

The fourth event is that graves that had held the bodies of many dead saints were cracked open, in preparation for their physical resurrection, which happened shortly after the Lord Himself had resurrected. *"They came out of the tombs after Jesus' resurrection and went into the holy city and appeared to many people"* (Matthew 27:53).

This clearly confirms that the purpose of Christ dying is so that we might live. I speak life to you today in the name of Jesus. I declare that every force or power that has kept you bound and confined for years be broken today, in the name of Jesus!

5
THE RESURRECTION AS THE CORNERSTONE OF OUR FAITH

"The resurrection is the pivot on which all of Christianity turns and without which none of the other truths would much matter. Without the resurrection, Christianity would be so much wishful thinking, taking its place alongside all other human philosophy and religious speculation."

– JOHN MACARTHUR

We saw earlier how the disciples, who had been so helpless and hopeless, suddenly became empowered and emboldened by their encounters with the risen Christ. You know what? That was the catalyst for the beginning of Christianity!

It happened that shortly after His glorious emergence from the grave, the Lord instructed His disciples to gather at Mount Olives. There, He gave them the most powerful assurance they had ever heard and instructed them to spread the good news of free salvation for all. He declared, *"All power is given unto me in heaven and in earth. Go ye therefore, and teach all nations, baptizing them in the name of the Father, and of the Son, and of the Holy Ghost: Teaching them to observe all things whatsoever I have commanded you: and, lo, I am with you alway, even unto the end of the world. Amen"* (Matthew 28:18-20, KJV).

Can you imagine that! As if it was not enough that He had just conquered death and humiliated both the Roman and the Jewish authorities! As if it was not enough that He had just rekindled and redoubled the hope and joy of His followers! He was now telling them that ALL POWER is given unto HIM!

Come on! Do you know what power means? It is the ability or capacity to do something or influence the course of events. And Jesus said ALL is given to Him, meaning that He can do all things and influence any course of event. And He said He was going to be with them all through their lives, as they obeyed the Great Commission He was giving to them.

That was all the disciples needed to be fired up with uncommon conviction and unstoppable zeal to spread the message of the resurrection everywhere at whatever cost. No wonder the Apostle John would later write: *"That which we have seen and heard declare we unto you, that ye also may have fellowship with us: and truly our fellowship is with the Father, and with his Son Jesus Christ. And these things write we unto you, that your joy may be full"* (1 John 1:3-4).

THE FIRST CHURCH

The apostles' joy was indeed full and their faith was supercharged, as they realized that there was nothing to limit or frighten them anymore. Death was conquered, shame was wiped off and hope was rejuvenated. Thus, immediately after they were baptized with the Holy Ghost (in Acts 2), they went into action in full force, with the same Peter who had fearfully denied the Savior, leading the charge. He declared to the same people who had earlier called for Christ's crucifixion: *"Fellow Israelites, listen to this: Jesus of Nazareth was a man accredited by God to you by miracles, wonders and signs, which God did among you through him, as you yourselves know. This man was handed over to you by God's deliberate plan and foreknowledge; and you, with the help of wicked men, put him to death by nailing him to the cross. But God raised him from the dead, freeing him from the agony of death, because it was impossible for death to keep its hold on him…"* (Acts 2:22-24).

From that powerful ministration, over 3000 people believed the gospel message and were saved and added to the number of the apostles. They too became proclaimers of the resurrection message and the blessings it offers. And, as the Scripture narrates, *"They devoted themselves to the* apostles' teaching and to fellowship, to the breaking of bread and to prayer. Everyone was filled with awe at the many wonders and signs performed by the apostles. All the believers were together and had everything in common. They sold property and possessions to give to anyone who had need. Every day they continued to meet together in the temple courts. They broke bread in their homes and ate together with glad and sincere hearts, praising God and enjoying the favor of all the people. And the Lord added to their number daily those who were being saved"* (Acts 2:42-47).

That, in a nutshell, is the history of Christianity and the church as we know it today. Simply put, it was the resurrection that birthed the church, the body of Christ established here on earth!

THE SOUL OF CHRISTIANITY

So, why did I lift that curtain of history as above? It is for you to know that the Christian faith is foundationally rooted and solidly hinged on the resurrection. In other words, without the resurrection, there is no Christianity. Michael Green puts it this way, *"Christianity does not hold the resurrection to be one among many tenets of belief. Without faith in the resurrection there would be no Christianity at all. The Christian church would never have begun; the Jesus-movement would have fizzled out like a damp squib with His execution. Christianity stands or falls with the truth of the resurrection. Once disprove it, and you have disposed of Christianity."*

I believe you will understand this truth better when you recall that the people who eventually became the pillars of the early church had initially scattered and lost hope, immediately after the death of Jesus Christ. Even Peter, upon whom Jesus said He would build the church (Matthew 16:18), had decided to return to his fishing business! What restored their hope and vision was the resurrection. It is for this reason that the resurrection constitutes the very soul of Christianity, the central truth of the Gospel!

What drove and kept the early believers on the firing line of the Gospel was the truth of the resurrection. As the "Bible Answer Man", Hank Hanegraaff, wrote: "What happened as a result of the resurrection is unprecedented in human history. In the span of a few hundred years, a small band of seemingly insignificant believers succeeded in turning an entire empire upside down. As has been well said, "They faced the tyrant's brandished steel, the lion's gory mane, and the fires of a thousand deaths," because they were utterly convinced that they, like their Master, would one day rise from the grave in glorified, resurrected bodies."

Even Paul the Apostle, who came in later on, could not stop cherishing and publishing the resurrection message. Of course, he had been one of the fiercest opponents of the Gospel and the early believers. But, from the moment he had that life-changing encounter with the risen Christ on the way to Damascus (Acts 9:1-9), all he could think of as his lifetime focus and preoccupation was the resurrection. According to him, *"I want to know Christ—yes, to know the power of his resurrection and participation in his sufferings, becoming like him in his death, and so, somehow, attaining to the resurrection from the dead. Not that I have already obtained all this, or have already arrived at my goal, but I press on to take hold of that for which Christ Jesus took hold of me"* (Philippians 3:10-14).

But why exactly is the resurrection so critical to the Christian faith?

1. The resurrection is what validates our faith.

The resurrection is the substance of our faith. It is what makes it meaningful – what shows that it is not in vain. Or of what meaning is a faith that offers no concrete hope of life after this brief stint on earth? Of what use is a faith whose founder's life was tragically, helplessly and hopelessly cut short in its prime?

Even more, how would we have been sure that God had accepted Christ's sacrifice for our salvation and redemption, if He had not returned from the grave to give us the much needed assurance? No wonder Paul wrote, *"Now if Christ be preached that he rose from the dead, how say some among you that there is no resurrection of the dead? But if there be no resurrection of the dead, then is Christ not risen: And if Christ be not risen, then is our preaching vain, and your faith is also vain. Yea, and we are found false witnesses of God; because we have testified of God that he raised up Christ: whom he raised not up, if so be that the dead rise not. For if the dead rise not, then is not Christ raised: And if Christ be not raised, your faith is vain; ye are yet in your sins. Then they also which are fallen asleep in Christ are perished. If in this life only we have hope in Christ, we are of all men most miserable"* (1 Corinthians 15:12-19, KJV).

Pastor Jim Eliff of Christian Communicators Worldwide offers this interesting perspective: *"If Jesus were not raised from the dead then we could not have assurance that the price of our sins has been paid. Christ was the perfect Lamb offered in our place, the single sufficient sacrifice for the sins of all who would believe on Him. His death provided our only way of being accepted by God. Without it we are doomed. Christ's resurrection is the assurance that this was completed, and that sin and its resulting death (physical and spiritual) was fully overthrown. What assurance could we have that the work promised had been done through the means of the cross if He did not rise to verify it?"*

2. The resurrection is what differentiates and elevates our faith.

The resurrection not only proves Christ's completed work of salvation but also validates His divinity and credibility. In other words, the resurrection shows that we are not just following a master, a teacher or a prophet, as adherents of other faiths claim – we are following the Son of God and, in fact, the very Source of Life Himself! Halleluiah!

The Apostle John testified of Christ, saying: "In him was life, and that life was the light of all mankind." (John 1:4). The Redeemer Himself said, *"The reason my Father loves me is that I lay down my life —only to take it up again. No one takes it from me, but I lay it down of my own accord. I have authority to lay it down and authority to take it up again…"* (John 10:17-18). At another time, He said, *"I am the resurrection and the life. He who believes in Me will live, even though he dies"* (John 11:25, NKJV). And also, *"I am the way, the truth, and the life: no man cometh unto the Father, but by me"* (John 14:6, KJV).

No other founder of a religion could make or prove these assertions about Himself, but Jesus did! He made many bold claims, such as calling himself the Son of God and saying that he had the authority to forgive sins. His resurrection confirms that these claims were not just empty words but were in fact true. Again, He said it was His prerogative to die, as well as to decide when He would die and when He would resurrect. No other leader could do this! Not only could they not predict when they would die but they all died and remain DEAD. Only Jesus Christ rose again.

There are an estimated 4000 religions, faiths groups, and denominations around the world, which are generally categorized into five major religious groups - Christianity, Islam, Buddhism, Hinduism, and Judaism. The founders of these other diverse faiths were probably good men while they lived. They might have touched lives and created movements. But Jesus Christ is in a class of His own. While He was on earth, He brought the Kingdom with Him and established it here! While others died and are still buried, Jesus died and resurrected! His tomb is empty! His ability to rise from the dead confers upon him the God status. It puts him head and shoulders above the founder of any other religion.

Here is Hank Hanegraaff again: "The resurrection is not merely important to the historic Christian faith; without it, there would be no Christianity. It is the singular doctrine that elevates Christianity above all other world religions. Through the resurrection, Christ demonstrated that He does not stand in a line of peers with Abraham, Buddha, or Confucius. He is utterly unique. He has the power not only to lay down His life, but to take it up again."

3. The resurrection is what gives power to our gospel.

Without the resurrection, the Gospel becomes like any other lifeless, man-made philosophy. The core of the Good News that we preach is Christ and His resurrection from the dead. The fact that our Savior does not need another person to raise him from the dead like other leaders but is alive for evermore makes our gospel distinctive in its appeal.

Apostle Paul boldly declared, "For I am not ashamed of

the gospel, because it is the power of God that brings salvation to everyone who believes: first to the Jew, then to the Gentile. For in the gospel the righteousness of God is revealed —a righteousness that is by faith from first to last, just as it is written: "The righteous will live by faith." (Romans 1:16-17). What is the source of this confidence and power? It is the resurrection and the compelling message it carries!

The message of redemption, hope, unlimited grace and eternal life that the resurrection carries makes it particularly perfect for every human need. It provides the solution to humanity's greatest problem—sin and its consequence, death. In other words, only the Gospel, through the resurrection message, guarantees the efficacy of God's redemption agenda for mankind! Only the gospel tells of the complete work of redemption for humanity. This is what has sustained the fervor and vigor in the dissemination of the gospel for so many centuries!

4. **The resurrection affirms the truth and reliability of Scripture.**

The resurrection adds another powerful layer of proof to the authenticity and reliability of the Scripture as God's word. 2 Timothy 3:16 says, "All Scripture is inspired by God…" and the resurrection totally proves this to be true. It will interest you to know that the books of the Bible were written by different authors from diverse backgrounds and occupations, over a very long period of time (about 1500 years). Most of these individuals never really met one another; yet, each had a theme, sign or prophecy about Jesus.

Specifically about Jesus' death and resurrection, there are several prophecies in the Old Testament, all of which predated even His birth! Take, for instance, the declaration by God, in Genesis 3:15, which we read earlier: *"And I will put enmity between thee and the woman, and between thy seed and her seed; it shall bruise thy head, and thou shalt bruise his heel."* Just in one verse, the birth, the death and the victory of Jesus through the resurrection were foretold by the everlasting God Himself and everything happened several generations later, just as He had said!

Also in Psalms 16:10, King David was inspired to prophesy, *"For you will not leave my soul among the dead or allow your holy one to rot in the grave"* (NLT). Obviously, David was not talking about himself here. As Apostle Peter recalled in his great sermon in Acts 2:29-36: *"Dear brothers, think about this! You can be sure that the patriarch David wasn't referring to himself, for he died and was buried, and his tomb is still here among us. But he was a prophet, and he knew God had promised with an oath that one of David's own descendants would sit on his throne. David was looking into the future and speaking of the Messiah's resurrection. He was saying that God would not leave him among the dead or allow his* body to rot in the grave. God raised Jesus from the dead, and we are all witnesses of this. Now he is exalted to the place of highest honor in heaven, at God's right hand. And the Father, as he had promised, gave him the Holy Spirit to pour out upon us, just as you see and hear today. For David himself never ascended into heaven, yet he said, 'The LORD said to my Lord, "Sit in the place of honor at my right hand until I humble your enemies, making them a footstool under your feet."' "So let everyone in Israel know for certain that God has made this Jesus, whom you crucified, to be both Lord and Messiah!"* (NLT).

There are several other pointers in both the Old and the New Testaments by different inspired writers, all which were confirmed by the resurrection. Jesus Himself affirmed this to the disciples on the way to Emmaus, as recorded in Luke 24:27: "Then Jesus took them through the writings of Moses and all the prophets, explaining from all the Scriptures the things concerning himself. "

This is awesome and it further solidifies our assurance in the truth and reliability of every part of Scripture. Indeed, *"every word of God is pure: he is a shield unto them that put their trust in him"* (Proverbs 30:5).

Beyond this reliability of the Scripture, however, there is something else I want you to notice here. The fact that the entire course of events surrounding the mission of Christ on earth - from His crucifixion to His death, from His burial to His resurrection - was already predicted in the Old Testament, shows that God is specific about every detail of our lives. Be sure of this - God is very specific about your life. He is intentional about every word that He has spoken about your life.

Therefore, I declare that, in this season, there will be a fulfilment of God's words in your life and in your family. As the Bible says in Isaiah 55:11, not one word that God has spoken over your life will return to Him void; every single word shall prosper and fulfil its purpose in your life, in the name of Jesus!

5. The resurrection caused the release of the Holy Ghost and power on the church.

The Holy Spirit is the power with which the church is able to successfully propagate the Gospel and fulfil the mandate of the Great Commission. Without the Holy Spirit, the church is lifeless, because everything the church does for impact – whether in ministration or administration - is powered by the Holy Spirit. However, the release of the Spirit's power and the power for diverse miracles on the church is closely attached to the glorious resurrection of Jesus Christ.

First of all, it was during one of His post-resurrection appearances to the disciples that Jesus "breathed on them and said, "Receive the Holy Spirit" (John 20:22). Again, it was during one of such appearances that He gave specific instructions on how the Holy Spirit would be released on the apostles. Acts 1:4-8 reveals that "On one occasion, while he was eating with them, he gave them this command: *'Do not leave Jerusalem, but wait for the gift my Father promised, which you have heard me speak about. For John baptized with water, but in a few days you will be baptized with the Holy Spirit."* Then they gathered around him and asked him, "Lord, are you at this time going to restore the kingdom to Israel?" He said to them: *"It is not for you to know the times or dates the Father has set by his own authority. But you will receive power when the Holy Spirit comes on you; and you will be my witnesses in Jerusalem, and in all Judea and Samaria, and to the ends of the earth."*

Peter, in his sermon on the day the Holy Spirit was released actually gave credit to Jesus and His resurrection, saying: *"God has raised this Jesus to life, and we are all witnesses of it. Exalted to the right hand of God, he has received from the Father the promised Holy Spirit and has poured out what you now see and hear"* (Acts 2:32-33).

As we have also seen, Paul, too, gave credit for the outpouring of the Holy Spirit and His gifts upon the church to the resurrection and ascension of Jesus. He declared, "But to each one of us grace has been given as Christ apportioned it. This is why it says: *'When he ascended on high, he took many captives and gave gifts to his people.'"*(What does "he ascended" mean except that he also descended to the lower, earthly regions? He who descended is the very one who ascended higher than all the heavens, in order to fill the whole universe.) So Christ himself gave the apostles, the prophets, the evangelists, the pastors and teachers, to equip his people for works of service, so that the body of Christ may be built up until we all reach unity in the faith and in the knowledge of the Son of God and become mature, attaining to the whole measure of the fullness of Christ." (Ephesians 4:7-13).

Did you notice that expression in the first statement – "as Christ apportioned it"? And when did He do the release and apportioning? "When he ascended". But before he ascended, He "descended to the lower, earthly regions"! Now, you see that all we do and the blessings we enjoy today as a church are the direct result of the resurrection. Praise God!

Let us now proceed to see the personal dimension of these glorious blessings of the resurrection!

6
THE RESURRECTION AND YOUR DOMINION

"The message of Easter is that God's new world has been unveiled in Jesus Christ and that you're now invited to belong to it."

- N. T. WRIGHT

While it is true that the blessings of Christ's resurrection are available to all humanity, it is also true that you cannot truly enjoy these blessings until you personalize them. Therefore, I will be devoting this chapter to letting you see the multitudes of blessings that have been made available to you through the resurrection.

First, let me remind you that one reason Jesus had to physically resurrect was to prove that the sacrifice he offered on the cross on your behalf was not only successfully completed, but also totally accepted by God. No wonder He declared, as He was about to die, "It is finished!" (John 19:30).

Yes, it is finished! The work of your salvation and redemption is finished. Everything you need to be happy, successful, prosperous and have dominion in all areas of life has been paid for and the price has been accepted by God. All that is left is for you to dive in and enjoy!

YOUR MULTIDIMENSIONAL POWER THROUGH THE RESURRECTION

Christ's resurrection was an unprecedented manifestation of God's mighty power. Thankfully, God has made that same power available to all who choose to accept the risen Christ into their lives. Once you fully understand how much power is accessible to you and consciously decide to appropriate it, you can be sure that everything about your life will never remain the same again.

This is why Paul wrote in Ephesians 1:19-23, *"I also pray that you will understand the incredible greatness of God's power for us who believe him. This is the same mighty power that raised Christ from the dead and seated him in the place of honor at God's right hand in the heavenly realms. Now he is far above any ruler or authority or power or leader or anything else—not only in this world but also in the world to come. God has put all things under the authority of Christ and has made him head over all things for the benefit of the church. And the church is his body; it is made full and complete by Christ, who fills all things everywhere with himself"* (NLT).

Let us unpack the different dimensions of this resurrection power that God has provided for you to function in.

1. POWER TO LIVE IN NEWNESS OF LIFE

Through the resurrection of Christ, you not only have access to salvation from sin and justification (Romans 10:9; 4:25) but also power to live in newness of life, which comes from the new birth (1 Peter 1:3). Colossians 2:11-12 reads, *"When you came to Christ, you were "circumcised," but not by a physical procedure. Christ performed a spiritual circumcision—the cutting away of your sinful nature. For you were buried with Christ when you were baptized. And with him you were raised to new life because you trusted the mighty power of God, who raised Christ from the dead"* (NLT).

Is this not glorious? With Christ's death and burial, the price for your sins —no matter how many or horrible they may be - has been paid and your sins have been buried with Him. But with Christ's resurrection, the power for you to become a totally new person has been made available. 2 Corinthians 5:17 says, *"...anyone who belongs to Christ has become a new person. The old life is gone; a new life has begun!"*

What this implies is that you can live above the guilt and condemnation of your past sins and you can also receive power to live above sin every day of your life through the grace of God (Romans 6:14, Titus 2:11-12). Let no one make you think that you are too far gone in sin to be redeemed, or that your habits and addictions are too strong for you to overcome. If you would sincerely call upon God to cleanse your sins with the blood of Jesus and then quicken you with the resurrection power that quickened Jesus from the grave, every chain that has held you bound will be broken and you will emerge with the triumphant power of the risen Christ.

"We were therefore buried with him through baptism into death in order that, just as Christ was raised from the dead through the glory of the Father, we too may live a new life…For we know that our old self was crucified with him so that the body ruled by sin might be done away with, that we should no longer be slaves to sin…" (Romans 6:4-6).

By the resurrection power of Jesus, you can be free from slavery to any kind of sinful habit or relationship and live the Christ-like life that you have been called to live. Through resurrection, you can literally feel and enjoy the presence of Christ and His power over sin in your everyday experience. Apostle Paul shared his own testimony thus: *"I have been crucified with Christ and I no longer live, but Christ lives in me. The life I now live in the body, I live by faith in the Son of God, who loved me and gave himself for me"* (Galatians 2:20). I pray this will be your testimony too!

2. POWER OVER PRINCIPALITIES AND POWERS

Apostle Paul, in his prayer for believers that we read earlier, declared that, following the resurrection, God has set Jesus Christ at His right hand, "far above all principality, and power, and might, and dominion, and every name that is named, not only in this world, but also in that which is to come. And hath put all things under his feet… (Ephesians 1:21-22, KJV). However, as if to emphasize and make it clearer to us where we belong in this new order, he disclosed in the very next chapter: *"But God, who is rich in mercy, for his great love wherewith he loved us, Even when we were dead in sins, hath quickened us together with Christ, (by grace ye are saved;) And hath raised us up together, and made us sit together in heavenly places in Christ Jesus"* (Ephesians 2:4-60).

What this means for you is that, if the same power that quickened Jesus from the grave has quickened you from your sins, then you occupy the same place of power and dominion that Jesus occupies in heaven. You have been repositioned to have authority over principalities and powers and all other forces of darkness, such that they recognize and tremble before you.

Paul himself was a living proof of this. When the seven sons of Sceva, who had not received the resurrected Christ into them, tried to cast out evil spirits, just as they had seen

Paul do, the result they got shocked and shook them. *"Some Jews who went around driving out evil spirits tried to invoke the name of the Lord Jesus over those who were demon-possessed. They would say, "In the name of the Jesus whom Paul preaches, I command you to come out."* Seven sons of Sceva, a Jewish chief priest, were doing this. One day the evil spirit answered them, *"Jesus I know, and Paul I know about, but who are you?" Then the man who had the evil spirit jumped on them and overpowered them all. He gave them such a beating that they ran out of the house naked and bleeding"* (Acts 19:13-16).

Did you see that powerful testimony from the evil spirit? He admitted recognizing the authority of Paul, just as he recognized that of Jesus. Why would he say that? Because the regenerated Paul was seated in the same place of unlimited dominion as the resurrected Christ!

Do you understand how much power you carry now, as a redeemed of the Lord? The Scripture says of the risen Christ, *"And having spoiled principalities and powers, he made a shew of them openly, triumphing over them in it"* (Colossians 2:15, KJV). Therefore, whether in the day or in the night, whether in the city or in the village, you have no reason to fear satanic attacks or demonic torment *"because greater is he that is in you, than he that is in the world"* (1 John 4:4).

3. POWER TO REVIVE AND TRANSMIT LIFE

The resurrection power is a quickening, life-giving power. No wonder 1 Corinthians 15:45 says: "The first man Adam became a living being"; the last Adam, a life-giving spirit." This life-giving spirit is what you have in you, as a child of God. This means that whatever or whoever you declare life into will come alive. Whatever you activate will be activated and whatever you deactivate will be deactivated.

How do you use this power? All around you are people living lifelessly and hopelessly. There are those who are spiritually dead and those who are physically dying. Many of these, like the Macedonians, are silently crying, "Come over… and help us." (Acts 16:9-10). With the resurrection power working in your life, you are the representative of Christ to these people. Transmit the same power to them to quicken their spirit, soul and body. Follow the instructions that God gave to Prophet Ezekiel in Ezekiel 37:4-6, *"Prophesy upon these bones, and say unto them, O ye dry bones, hear the word of the LORD. Thus saith the Lord GOD unto these bones; Behold, I will cause breath to enter into you, and ye shall live: And I will lay sinews upon you, and will bring up flesh upon you, and cover you with skin, and put breath in you, and ye shall live; and ye shall know that I am the LORD"* (KJV).

Everywhere you go, let your testimony be like that of Jesus in Matthew 4:15-16, *"The land of Zabulon, and the land of Nephthalim, by the way of the sea, beyond Jordan, Galilee of the Gentiles; The people which sat in darkness saw great light; and to them which sat in the region and shadow of death light is sprung up."*

You can personally use this life-giving power to quicken and call forth your blessings and any other good thing that belongs to you that seems to be dying or dormant. Call forth your breakthrough, promotion, business ideas, healing and whatever you wish to see manifest.

POWER FOR SUPERNATURAL SIGNS AND WONDERS

Beyond dispensing life, the resurrection power that is functioning in you is an all-round miracle-working power. The Scripture reveals that, as the risen Christ gave the disciples the mandate of the Great Commission, He also added that, with all power now given to Him, the power for diverse miracles will be manifested by all who receive Him. He declared, *"And these signs will follow those who believe: In My name they will cast out demons; they will speak with new tongues; they will take up serpents; and if they drink anything deadly, it will by no means hurt them; they will lay hands on the sick, and they will recover"* (Mark 16:17-18).

If you are among those who have received Christ, then your life must perpetually reflect these signs and wonders. In fact, the Messiah had earlier declared that *"Verily, verily, I say unto you, He that believeth on me, the works that I do shall he do also; and greater works than these shall he do; because I go unto my Father"* (John 14:12). How many great works did Christ perform that you can remember? I am sure there are many. But He is saying here that not only have you been empowered to continue from where He stopped but also equipped to even do more!

What happened through the apostles, soon after the risen Lord had ascended to heaven, confirms that all believers have this dimension of the resurrection power in them. Acts 3, for instance reveals that Peter and John healed a man that had been crippled from birth by a simple command with the name of Jesus (Acts 3:1-8). The Scripture further reveals that *"by the hands of the apostles were many signs and wonders wrought among the people…Insomuch that they brought forth the sick into the streets, and laid them on beds and couches, that at the least the shadow of Peter passing by might overshadow some of them. There came also a multitude out of the cities round about unto Jerusalem, bringing sick folks, and them which were vexed with unclean spirits: and they were healed every one."* (Acts 5:12-16).

The last line there is particularly interesting. It says that every case that was brought to the disciples got a solution. That is how POTENT the resurrection power that works in you is – it knows no limitation or impossibility!

4. POWER TO CONQUER OBSTACLES AND OPPOSITIONS

Matthew 28:2, in narrating the resurrection story, says: *"And, behold, there was a great earthquake: for the angel of the Lord descended from heaven, and came and rolled back the stone from the door, and sat upon it."* Halleluiah! The resurrection power at work in your life is one that is unstoppable! Remember that the grave of Jesus had been barricaded with a huge stone. However, as soon as the resurrection power got in motion, nothing could stop the Lord from coming out of the grave.

By the power of the resurrection available to you, no barrier or opposition can hinder you from fulfilling your purpose and destiny. You are destined for the top and no opposition can hinder your exaltation. As you activate the resurrection power in you, no enchantment can frustrate your enthronement. No manipulation can prevent your manifestation. You will become all that God has destined you to become by the power of the risen Christ. If no tomb could keep Jesus, no power can keep you bound because Christ in you is the hope of glory! (Colossians 1:27).

5. POWER TO SUBDUE EVERY ENEMY IN YOUR DAILY LIFE

Something else happened at the resurrection that you need to pay attention to. Here is the Matthew account again, *"And, behold, there was a great earthquake: for the angel of the Lord descended from heaven, and came and rolled back the stone from the door, and sat upon it. His countenance was like lightning, and his raiment white as snow: And for fear of him the keepers did shake, and became as dead men"* (Matthew 28:2-4).

The power that raised Jesus from the dead not rolled away the stone from His tomb but also disarmed His enemies. These enemies who were closely guarding the tomb, thinking they could hinder access to the tomb were subdued and paralyzed by the resurrection power, such that they "became as dead men".

Not only that, Philippians 2:8-11, speaking of Jesus, says: *"And being found in fashion as a man, he humbled himself, and became obedient unto death, even the death of the cross. Wherefore God also hath highly exalted him, and given him a name which is above every name: That at the name of Jesus every knee should bow, of things in heaven, and things in earth, and things under the earth; And that every tongue should confess that Jesus Christ is Lord, to the glory of God the Father."*

The assurance is that, as you call the exalted name of the resurrected Christ against every enemy, they will be subdued before you and they will admit that Jesus is Lord, indeed. You have the power to incapacitate every Pharaoh that has sworn to keep you from progressing and every Haman that is conspiring to keep you down or get you hanged. *"How blessed you are, O Israel! Who else is like you, a people saved by the LORD? He is your protecting shield and your triumphant sword! Your enemies will cringe before you, and you will stomp on their backs!"* (Deuteronomy 33:29, NLT)

6. POWER FOR WELLNESS OF BODY AND SOUNDNESS OF MIND

Romans 8:11 assures that "if the Spirit of him who raised Jesus from the dead is living in you, he who raised Christ from the dead will also give life to your mortal bodies because of his Spirit who lives in you." The same power that quickened the body of Jesus from the grave is very much available in you and must be activated to give life and wellness to every part of your body.

By the resurrection power, every part of your body must function healthily and optimally. Every cell, tissue or organ in your body must respond to the resurrection power. There must be no barrenness or impotence, and you must be daily rejuvenated. Indeed, by the power of the risen Christ, *"as your days, so shall your strength be"!* (Deuteronomy 33:25, NKJV).

The resurrection power also helps to quicken your mind for innovative productivity and creativity. 2 Timothy 1:7 says God has not given you the spirit of fear "but of power, and of love, and of a sound mind" (KJV).

7. POWER TO CONQUER LIMITATIONS AND EXCEED EXPECTATIONS

A major highlight of the resurrection power is its transformational effect. It shatters natural laws and limitations and replaces them with the supernatural. That was exactly what happened with the apostles and that is what will happen to you as you begin to activate the power in your life. Take, for example, Peter and John. Acts 4:13 reveals that *"when they saw the courage of Peter and John and realized that they were unschooled, ordinary men, they were astonished and they took note that these men had been with Jesus."*

Apparently, considering the social and educational background of Peter and John, nobody had expected them to amount to much in life. But since it was the resurrection power that was at work in them, their lives became a wonder, and people concluded that they must have been with Jesus.

You also have this power to make your life a testimony to the omnipotence of the risen Christ. I don't know what bad things that have been said about you, or how many people have written you off, or what negative outcomes people are expecting from your life. But by reason of your relationship with the risen Christ and by virtue of His power that is operational in you, you will exceed every expectation and become a wonder to your generation!

8. POWER FOR UNLIMITED IMPACT IN THE WORLD AND GOD'S KINGDOM

When the risen Christ gave us the charge to go and spread the gospel, He promised to be with us everywhere we go in obedience to His command. And to show the reliability of this promise, Mark 16:19-20 says, *"So then after the Lord had spoken unto them, he was received up into heaven, and sat on the right hand of God. And they went forth, and preached every where, the Lord working with them, and confirming the word with signs following. Amen."*

What does this tell you?" You have the power for unlimited impact in the world around you as you go about preaching the Good News. The awareness that the risen Lord is ever with you should fill you with unwavering courage like the early apostles!

Similarly, the Scripture reveals that, as He ascended to heaven, the risen Christ distributed gifts for the building up of His church for greater execution of the Kingdom mandate. These gifts are available to empower you for greater usefulness and fruitfulness in God's Kingdom. Seek them earnestly and you will be filled!

9. POWER TO BE KEPT IN FAITH FOR ETERNAL GLORY

This is the ultimate effect of the operation of the resurrection power in your life. According to 1 Peter 1:3-6, *"Praise be to the God and Father of our Lord Jesus Christ! In his great mercy he has given us new birth into a living hope through the resurrection of Jesus Christ from the dead, and into an inheritance that can never perish, spoil or fade. This inheritance is kept in heaven for you, who through faith are shielded by God's power until the coming of the salvation that is ready to be revealed in the last time."*

Now that you know the extent of the power you can exercise and enjoy through Christ's resurrection, it is time to begin to activate this power and live your daily life in consciousness of the dominion you have in the risen Christ!

7
THE RESURRECTION AND OUR ETERNAL GLORY

"Time is short. Eternity is long. It is only reasonable that this short life be lived in the light of eternity."

- C. H. SPURGEON

This is undoubtedly the greatest blessing that the resurrection of Christ offers to us – the concrete and unshakeable guarantee that someday we all will be raised up to reign with Christ forever! Praise God!

This truth alone brings a greater dimension of meaning, purpose and vigor to our present life. This is so because regardless of the joys and triumphs we enjoy through the resurrection in this world, our earthly life is still like "a vapor that appears for a little time and then vanishes away" (James 4:14). Besides, even this brief time is sometimes rocked by moments of sadness and despair, which the grace of God, through the resurrection power, helps us to overcome.

Now, would it not be so miserable and meaningless, if this were all there is to life? If life were to be all about the brief time we spend on earth and the various battles fought and the victories won? Certainly so, because there would always be uncertainty about when and how everything would end, and what would happen to us and all we had labored for afterwards. No wonder, Paul the Apostle declared, *"If in this life only we have hope in Christ, we are of all men most miserable"* (1 Corinthians 15:19, KJV).

COMFORT FROM THE RESURRECTION

Thankfully, however, through the truth of the resurrection, as well as the multitudes of assurances we have from the Scripture and the proof of concept (POC) that our Lord Himself demonstrated, we know that there is so much more to life than what we have on earth. The resurrection, in particular, proves to us that death is no longer an enemy to be feared but a passageway to be joyfully embraced for a far greater and more glorious life for us after life on earth.

Hebrews 2:14-15 specifically says of Christ's death and resurrection, *"Inasmuch then as the children have partaken of flesh and blood, He Himself likewise shared in the same, that through death He might destroy him who had the power of death, that is, the devil, and release those who through fear of death were all their lifetime subject to bondage"* (NKJV).

Jesus has conquered the fear of death, alongside the devil, who used to have the power of death. Death to us therefore is not a termination of life but a transition to eternal glory and an everlasting inheritance. As 1 Peter 1:3-6 further reveals: *"Praise be to the God and Father of our Lord Jesus Christ! In his great mercy he has given us new birth into a living hope through the resurrection of Jesus Christ from the dead, and into an inheritance that can never perish, spoil or fade. This inheritance is kept in heaven for you, who through faith are shielded by God's power until the coming of the salvation that is ready to be revealed in the last time. In all this you greatly rejoice, though now for a little while you may have had to suffer grief in all kinds of trials."*

Again, this is one reason why the resurrection elevates our faith and bolsters our hope above that of followers of other religions or even science. While a few other religions out there make mention of the afterlife, their allusions are vague and offer little or no hope, as there is no concrete proof from their founders that there is life after death. And those who trust in science are in a more serious dilemma, as it offers no definitive proof of life after death for them.

Only Jesus, by His resurrection, has provided a powerful and compelling proof that there is a certainty of life eternal for all who follow Him. As the late Scottish-American preacher, Peter Marshall, explained, *"No tabloid will ever print the startling news that the mummified body of Jesus of Nazareth has been discovered in old Jerusalem. Christians have no carefully* embalmed body enclosed in a glass case to worship. Thank God, we have an empty tomb. The glorious fact that the empty tomb proclaims to us is that life for us does not stop when death comes. Death is not a wall, but a door."

GUARANTEES OF FINAL RESURRECTION AND ETERNAL LIFE

Even before His death and resurrection, Christ frequently made it clear that anyone who accepts Him not only enjoys abundant life on earth but also an eternal life that can never be terminated by death. He declared in John 11:25-26, *"I am the resurrection and the life. He who believes in Me, though he may die, he shall live. And whoever lives and believes in Me shall never die…"*

What an uplifting assurance! Believers in Christ do not die; we simply step up into our glorious bodies and heavenly home! The Lord again affirmed this, saying: *"Let not your heart be troubled; you believe in God, believe also in Me. In My Father's house are many mansions; if it were not so, I would have told you. I go to prepare a place for you. And if I go and prepare a place for you, I will come again and receive you to Myself; that where I am, there you may be also"* (John 14:1-3).

When Jesus resurrected, the disciples' faith became more reinforced in these assurances. It settled it for them that Jesus indeed is the source of life and having Him automatically means having a life that can never die or be threatened by the fear of death. Essentially, through His resurrection, Jesus provided the best proof of concept (POC) for the doctrine of final resurrection and eternal life for believers.

In various aspects of human endeavor, POC is a demonstration or an experiment used to validate or test the feasibility or reliability of a particular idea or concept. It usually serves as a preliminary step before investing significant resources into the full-scale development or implementation of a project. In the context of the final resurrection and eternal life for believers, Jesus seemed to first show us the validity of the doctrine by resurrecting different people at different stages of death. These include Jairus' daughter, who had just died (Luke 8:41-56), and Lazarus, who had died for four days and was already decaying (John 11). Then He completed it all by doing it in Himself! *"Jesus answered them, "Destroy this temple, and I will raise it again in three days." They replied, "It has taken forty-six years to build this temple, and you are going to raise it in three days?" But the temple he had spoken of was his body. After he was raised from the dead, his disciples recalled what he had said. Then they believed the scripture and the words that Jesus had spoken"* (John 2:19-22).

No wonder, the early apostles had a radical change in their perspective of death – so much that they resorted to using the term "fell asleep" to describe dying (See Acts 7:60, 1 Corinthians 15:6, 20 and 1 Thessalonians 4:13-18 for examples). Interestingly, it was the same expression that the Lord Himself had often used to describe the death of those dear to Him (see the cases of Lazarus and Jairus' daughter). The reason is simple - sleep implies a peaceful and temporary state, as opposed to the finality and darkness that is often associated with death. The purpose is to emphasize that death is not the end for believers, but merely a temporary rest before they are awakened to a new and eternal life!

SURE ANCHOR IN LIFE'S STORMS

The early believers held firmly to the assurances of eternal life by the Lord amidst the diverse tribulations and persecutions that they faced, and they frequently used it to encourage one another. In 1 John 5:11-13, for example, the Apostle echoed what Christ had told them: *"And this is the record, that God hath given to us eternal life, and this life is in his Son. He that hath the Son hath life; and he that hath not the Son of God hath not life. These things have I written unto you that believe on the name of the Son of God; that ye may know that ye have eternal life…"* (KJV).

Earlier on, Apostle Paul wrote to encourage the Thessalonians, who were struggling to cope with the loss of their loved ones, *"But I do not want you to be ignorant, brethren, concerning those who have fallen asleep, lest you sorrow as others who have no hope. For if we believe that Jesus died and rose again, even so God will bring with Him those who sleep in Jesus. For this we say to you by the word of the Lord, that we who are alive and remain until the coming of the Lord will by no means precede those who are asleep. For the Lord Himself will descend from heaven with a shout, with the voice of an archangel, and with the trumpet of God. And the dead in Christ will rise first. Then we who are alive and remain shall be caught up together with them in the clouds to meet the Lord in the air. And thus we shall always be with the Lord. Therefore comfort one another with these words".* (1 Thessalonians 4:13-18, KJV).

Paul also wrote to the Corinthians, *"Behold, I tell you a mystery: We shall not all sleep, but we shall all be changed— in a moment, in the twinkling of an eye, at the last trumpet. For the trumpet will sound, and the dead will be raised incorruptible, and we shall be changed. For this corruptible must put on incorruption, and this mortal must put on immortality. So when this corruptible has put on incorruption, and this mortal has put on immortality, then shall be brought to pass the saying that is written: "Death is swallowed up in victory"* (1 Corinthians 15:51-54).

GLIMPSES OF OUR ETERNAL INHERITANCE

While we bask in the hope of the glorious life that awaits us in heaven when the present one is ended (whether by death or Christ's return), it is important we have some insight into what this next life looks like. This, aside from strengthening our hope and further banishing our fear of death, will help us to better appreciate what Christ has achieved for us by His death and resurrection. Here are a few glimpses:

1. We will be changed.

Whether we leave this world by death or the rapture, one thing is certain – we are doing away with our present body and all its weaknesses, limitations and vulnerabilities, in exchange for a perfect, glorious and heavenly body.

"Listen, I tell you a mystery: We will not all sleep, but we will all be changed — in a flash, in the twinkling of an eye, at the last trumpet. For the trumpet will sound, the dead will be raised imperishable, and we will be changed. For the perishable must clothe itself with the imperishable, and the mortal with immortality. When the perishable has been clothed with the imperishable, and the mortal with immortality, then the saying that is written will come true: 'Death has been swallowed up in victory.'" (1 Corinthians 15:51-54).

"But our citizenship is in heaven. And we eagerly await a Savior from there, the Lord Jesus Christ, who, by the power that enables him to bring everything under his control, will transform our lowly bodies so that they will be like his glorious body" (Philippians 3:20-21. See also 2 Corinthians 5:1).

2. We will be comforted and have fullness of peace and joy.

"And I heard a loud voice from the throne saying, 'Look! God's dwelling place is now among the people, and he will dwell with them.

They will be his people, and God himself will be with them and be their God. 'He will wipe every tear from their eyes. There will be no more death' or mourning or crying or pain, for the old order of things has passed away." (Revelation 21:3-4).

3. We will enjoy worshipping God with other saints.

"After this I looked, and there before me was a great multitude that no one could count, from every nation, tribe, people and language, standing before the throne and before the Lamb. They were wearing white robes and were holding palm branches in their hands. And they cried out in a loud voice: "Salvation belongs to our God, who sits on the throne, and to the Lamb." (Revelation 7:9-10).

4. We will no longer witness evil and wickedness.

"Nothing impure will ever enter it, nor will anyone who does what is shameful or deceitful, but only those whose names are written in the Lamb's book of life." (Revelation 21:27).

5. We will receive eternal rewards and reign with God forever.

"Praise be to the God and Father of our Lord Jesus Christ! In his great mercy he has given us new birth into a living hope through the resurrection of Jesus Christ from the dead, and into an inheritance that can never perish, spoil or fade. This inheritance is kept in heaven for you, 5 who through faith are shielded by God's power until the coming of the salvation that is ready to be revealed in the last time." (1 Peter 1:3-5),

"No longer will there be any curse. The throne of God and of the Lamb will be in the city, and his servants will serve him. They will see his face, and his name will be on their foreheads. There will be no more night. They will not need the light of a lamp or the light of the sun, for the Lord God will give them light. And they will reign for ever and ever." (Revelation 22:3-5).

Looking at all these glorious assurances, it is no wonder that the Scripture declares "Blessed are the dead who die in the Lord from now on…they will rest from their labor, for their deeds will follow them." (Revelation 14:13). It is also for this reason that many believers in both Bible times and the contemporary era embraced the approach of death with such peace and joy.

Here, for example, is how the Bible describes Stephen's death: "But Stephen, full of the Holy Spirit, looked up to heaven and saw the glory of God, and Jesus standing at the right hand of God. "Look," he said, *"I see heaven open and the Son of Man standing at the right hand of God."* At this they covered their ears and, yelling at the top of their voices, they all rushed at him, dragged him out of the city and began to stone him. Meanwhile, the witnesses laid their coats at the feet of a young man named Saul. While they were stoning him, Stephen prayed, *"Lord Jesus, receive my spirit."* Then he fell on his knees and cried out, *"Lord, do not hold this sin against them."* When he had said this, he fell asleep." (Acts 7:55-60).

Apostle Paul, too, once confidently told the Philippians: *"For to me, to live is Christ and to die is gain...I am torn between the two: I desire to depart and be with Christ, which is better by far; but it is more necessary for you that I remain in the body."* (Philippians 1:21-24). When the time eventually came for him to be killed as a soldier of Christ, he happily wrote to Timothy, his spiritual son, *"For I am already being poured out like a drink offering, and the time for my departure is near. I have fought the good fight, I have finished the race, I have kept the faith. 8 Now there is in store for me the crown of righteousness, which the Lord, the righteous Judge, will award to me on that day —and not only to me, but also to all who have longed for his appearing"* (2 Timothy 4:6-8).

What blessed assurance and hope it gives to know that because our Savior conquered death and resurrected, we have been redeemed and repositioned for a blessed life on earth and a blissful reign in heaven. Because Christ lives, we understand that, unlike others, our lives can never end. Whenever and in whichever way we depart this earth, it is not the end but the beginning of greater joys. As Phillips Brooks rightly said, let every believer in Christ consider himself (or herself) immortal. "Let him catch the revelation of Jesus in his resurrection. Let him say not merely, "Christ is risen," but "I shall rise!"

CONCLUSION
YOU ARE THE FIFTH GOSPEL!

What a great and glorious journey of revelations we have had so far on the inexhaustible benefits of Christ's resurrection. Not only do we have clearer insights into the blessedness of the resurrection of Jesus but also deeper understanding of the manifold provisions and privileges that are ours through the experience. In all, we are assured that, that even in our darkest moments there is always hope for renewal, redemption, and new beginnings for us. We know that, because Jesus has won the victory, we have victory!

Therefore, if you have not accepted Jesus Christ into your life yet, I invite you to surrender your life to Him today. He took on all the afflictions and sufferings, died on the cross and rose again, so you will no longer be bound by sin or afflicted by Satan. And if you have made Christ your Lord already, I enjoin you to continue on the path of salvation, so you will not be crucifying Christ again through sinful living.

Beyond that, it is important to remember that the writers of each of the four Gospels (Matthew, Mark, Luke and John) provided unique individual accounts of the resurrection of Jesus Christ. Now, you and I are the fifth Gospel. We have been commissioned and empowered to tell the world and resound the truth about the resurrection! The angels told the women at the tomb to proclaim the good news of the resurrection. Jesus also charged the disciples to spread the good news. Don't keep the resurrection message to yourself,; spread the inherent message of salvation and hope to your friends, family and everyone else you come across. Let them know that God loves them and wants to redeem them to Himself.

There are still multitudes around the world who are blinded to the light of the Gospel and consequently devoid of the uplifting assurance that the resurrection of Christ gives for this life and the afterlife. This why many are confused, anxious, depressed and sometimes suicidal. In fact, statistics show that every year, close to 800,000 people die by suicide. This means that there is a suicide every 40 seconds, and for each suicide, there are an estimated more than 20 suicide attempts. What a tragic picture!

The bulk of this tragedy comes from people having unanswered questions about life and being unable to see light at the end of the tunnel of life's challenges. For us in Christ, however, we have answers to these question, as well as the necessary encouragement to navigate the complexities of life, through the resurrection message. No wonder Jesus says we are the light of the world! And now is the time we must spread this gospel light with even greater intensity.

The same powerful charge that the Lord gave to all who witnessed His resurrection is what He is giving you and me today. We must spread the message of hope, light and life eternal that the resurrection brings to the dark, dreary and despairing world around us. As Ravi Zacharias rightly noted, "Outside of the cross of Jesus Christ, there is no hope in this world. That cross and resurrection at the core of the Gospel is the only hope for humanity."

www.ingramcontent.com/pod-product-compliance
Lightning Source LLC
LaVergne TN
LVHW051846080426
835512LV00018B/3098